GIVERS, TAKERS, AND OTHER KINDS OF LOVERS

# Givers, Takers and other kinds of Lovers

**JOSH McDOWELL**
**and Paul Lewis**

KINGSWAY PUBLICATIONS
EASTBOURNE

ISBN 0 86065 108 8

Unless otherwise indicated biblical quotations
are from the New American Standard Version.
Quotations from John White, *Eros Defiled*, are used
by permission of Inter-Varsity Press, Leicester (UK)
and Downers Grove (USA).

Printed in Great Britain for
KINGSWAY PUBLICATIONS LTD
Lottbridge Drove, Eastbourne, E. Sussex BN23 6NT by
Richard Clay (The Chaucer Press) Ltd, Bungay, Suffolk
Typesetting by Nuprint Services Ltd, Harpenden, Herts.

# CONTENTS

*To*
*Jim and Vivian Simpson*
*who have enjoyed and shared*
*the secret of loving for*
*thirty-eight years*

# 1

## *What Kind of Love Do You Want?*

Rich...vigorous...enduring and satisfying *love*! You want it. I want it. Without it, our lives are at best incomplete—at worst, desperate. The yearning to give and receive robust, unending love throbs in the heart of every one of us.

Years ago a Jewish apostle described this love we seek. He wrote:

> Love is so patient and so kind;
> Love never boils with jealousy;
> It never boasts, is never puffed with pride;
> It does not act with rudeness, or insist upon its rights;
> It never gets provoked, it never harbors evil thoughts;
> Is never glad when wrong is done,
> But always glad when truth prevails;
> It bears up under anything,
> It exercises faith in everything,
> It keeps up hope in everything,
> It gives us power to endure in anything.
> Love never fails. [1](1 Cor. 13:4-8, Williams)

And after two thousand more years of loving, no one has improved on that. It's still the love for which we search.

This pursuit of love has caused more heartache and pain than all the diseases and wars of history. There's no limit to what you and I will do to express true love...and to feel it for ourselves. We can't live without it.

Unfortunately, we don't seem able to live *with* it either. At least not with the sort of love we've found thus far. The prevailing notion is that love comes gift-wrapped in sex. And sex does seem to be the perfect complement—the door to genuine, satisfying love. What better bedfellows? Both sex and love stir the marvellous passions that lie deep within us.

Lovers come in an incredibly wide assortment. And why not? To some, love is an intricate and challenging game of strategy, and they're busy learning all the rules. Some become real polished players. Others are still looking for the square marked 'start'. And you? You're in there somewhere.

Several years ago I met Paul Lewis when we happened to be going out with twin sisters. Our friendship has been a deep and enduring one. It was at the time we met that we both began to recognize and understand what real love is all about. For us, those sisters and their parents modelled a love anyone would envy. That's why this book is dedicated to Mum and Dad Simpson.

In time Paul married one of those sisters, Leslie. Eleven years of marriage have deepened their understanding of how to keep and nourish true love. That's why I asked Paul to join me in writing this book.

Similarly, I have enjoyed a creative and beautiful relationship with my wife over the last nine years.

People try in many ways to discover this rich, vigorous and constantly growing love. Often we are persuaded that the secret is to become liberated and free from the puritanical restraints of the past. Well, I'm pleased to announce that we've all been free for quite a while. Even the memory of those repressive days has evaporated.

But I receive letters from all over the country, from young people as well as married adults, indicating that dynamic love is still missing for them. The yearning still burns unfulfilled. Maybe it's that way for you too. And shouldn't we ask why? Why, amid the unlimited freedom for sexual expression we've now enjoyed for so long, are we still as dissatisfied and unfulfilled as ever? Why is something so natural and beautiful as sex turning out such poor relationships?

What's wrong? Is sex not the secret of loving?

# 2

# Whatever Happened to Sexual Freedom?

Two years ago *Time* magazine printed a cartoon to illustrate a feature article on 'the new morality'. The cartoon showed two young women obviously involved in heavy conversation as they walked through a park. One woman said to the other, 'To tell the truth, I wish I'd been born before sex.'

While it's an extreme comment, as well as an amusing one, there are fleeting moments when every one of us feels like that. We are bombarded with an overload of information on sex. From dawn till dusk, the images and words—some subtle, some blatant—blast away at us. Whatever magazine you read, you're likely to find an article on sex. In one you can read about 'the pleasures of sexual freedom' and 'the problems of sexual freedom'. In another, a female clinical psychologist discusses 'the sexual loneliness of the male'. And if that doesn't turn you on, the next issue will have a male clinical psychologist telling women about 'self-confidence and sex appeal'. We can read 'how important is sex in marriage?' or 'getting more joy out of sex'. Single, married, old, young—sex is for us!

Television and films rub in the same message. Whether it's the suggestive shows, sexually-based advertisements for cars or romantic aftershave ('It arouses more than just your face'), the message is clear. Sexual freedom.

Writers and readers, producers and viewers—all are concerned with sexual liberty, sexual fulfilment, sexual pleasure, sexual fears, and sexual joys. The famous authorities, Masters and Johnson, have an organization geared totally to sex research. And other investigators with less scientific methods and more sensual conclusions flood the market with books which describe the latest 'love' techniques and body positions.

But sexual discussions aren't confined to print or films and television screens. Wherever people gather they talk sex—in homes, colleges, hotel rooms and cars. And despite all the comments and questions, the 'answers' are often fuzzy and tentative.

With all the emphasis on sex, researchers have had a field day. Pollsters have learned that more and more unmarried couples are living together—more people are having sexual intercourse outside of marriage than ever before, and they're doing it at a younger age. What was a good-night kiss twenty years ago has today become an evening of full disclosure. All this talk, freedom and experimentation has put the pressure on young people to perform.

For some, increased sexual awareness has been liberating. For others, it's become downright devastating.

Among the 'liberated' is Catherine Breslin, author of *The Mistress Condition: New Options in Sex, Love and Other Female Pleasures*. 'Sex,' she says, 'is certainly a large part of the new game—rollicking, satisfying, non-exploitative sex, a grownup but playful sort of business.' This 'game' is self-fulfilment and gratification. The 'new woman', she says, looks at life and sex from a different perspective from her older counterpart. To the new lady marriage 'looks like a strange and difficult, even burdensome arrangement'. One man can't meet all her needs. Says Breslin,

> A mistress-of-her-own-life may have eight or ten important men she enjoys: One for jogging in the park, one for the opera, another for skiing, still another for gourmet cooking, and two or three for good sex, each of them a different sensual experience. Plus two or three good, loving friends—men she can tell anything to, and cry all over when times get rough.

What about this perspective? Does it produce happiness and fulfilment? Does sex as a game and a 'playful business' generate a sense of personal worth? Does having many men dissolve the reality of loneliness or take the place of a permanent, enduring relationship?

According to the research, the answer is no. Says Theodore Rubin,

> Women often engage in sexual activity for non-sexual reasons. A woman goes out with a man and then goes to bed with him not because she wants to but because she feels that sex is expected and that she won't hear from him again unless she does. Sexual activity engaged in for this reason can make a woman feel unhappy—angry and guilty and used. If people engage in sex freely when they're not ready to, before they have sufficient self-esteem to decide whether they want to do it with a particular person or simply because they're told it's okay, that can lead to an increase in self-hate.

Feelings of anger, guilt and being used—consumed with self-hatred—are these the side-effects of liberation? Rubin is not the only one who is putting out warning signals. Clinical psychologist Lonnie Garfield Barbach, author of *For Yourself: The Fulfilment of Female Sexuality*, admits that the pressure may be greatest on younger women. Many of Barbach's patients feel that everyone is supposed to be 'free, open, sensual, multi-orgasmic and without sexual inhibition'. When they can't fulfil these expectations, they are 'incredibly hard on themselves'. She says, 'These women in their twenties are torn between the rather conservative messages their parents whisper to them and the philosophy of the sexual revolution.'

But it's not only the women who suffer. Dr Karen Shanor, a clinical psychologist who studied male sexuality for two years and published her findings in *The Shanor Study*, says, 'Like the American woman, the American man is currently re-examining his traditional image [which, she says, is to function as the conquering stud, and so on] and finding that it severely limits his potential as a human being.' More than half the men Shanor surveyed admitted that far from enjoying themselves, they were dissatisfied with their sex lives.

> Why? There were many reasons, but I can sum up by saying that all too often…men are caught in a no-man's land between the myth that no longer holds true (if, indeed, it ever did) and the dream that has not yet come true—the dream of a loving intimacy never to be achieved in a one-night stand. Men are, in a sense, on a journey from a bad place to a better one, but they have not yet reached their goal, and they are becoming increasingly conscious of the loneliness of the road.

Pop psychologist Dr Joyce Brothers commented on this sexual pilgrimage in the *Time* magazine look at the 'the new morality'. Brothers said, 'We're not as swinging a people as we think we are. People found that instant sex was about as satisfying as a sneeze. It takes a lot of time and trouble to have sex with a lot of people, and they found it wasn't even worth the scheduling.' Barbara Seaman, author of *Free and Female*, is even more descriptive:

> The backlash is against casual sex because a lot of people were hurt. It was as if there was a train gradually carrying us away from Victorian morality, but then suddenly in the 60s and 70s the train became a runaway and a lot of passengers were injured. Now the brakes are starting to be repaired.

One person who got derailed, but not seriously injured (her diagnosis), was Gretchen Kurz. A student at an American University, Gretchen talked very candidly in the August 1977 issue of *Mademoiselle* magazine. Says Gretchen, who entered university ready for the 'decadent life':

> There I was, well equipped with my pencil, student card and an adequate supply of birth control pills. But somehow, I missed the boat on the pleasure cruise to carefree, guiltfree sex. Actually, I now believe it's all a myth perpetuated by a lot of disappointed students too afraid to tell the truth. But then again, how are you supposed to admit it's all a crock after you couldn't wait to get out and break all the rules?

Gretchen never doubted that when she got to university she'd 'share' sex. But she says,

> To put it mildly, 'share' was a gross misnomer. My first encounter with Mr Variety-Is-the-Spice-of-Life left me utterly confused by a number of things. Do I leave now

or spend the night? What will I say in the morning? Is it kosher to borrow his bathrobe? Was I any good? He wasn't. Does this mean we've started something somewhat permanent?

She discovered it didn't.

To say that I was overcome by guilt would be a lie, but the experience was far from euphoric. The most positive description I could use to label the exchange would be 'dull'. It was void of emotion, or perhaps any trace of emotion was deftly disguised as avant-garde nonchalance. I soon found this cool and detached approach characteristic of any future encounters.

This lack of emotion not only baffled me, it infuriated me. I wanted to know why it existed and why it was so instrumental in the sexual liberation of my college friends. Obviously, it was the all too common basis for an active sex life.

Disturbed, Gretchen began to ask the many men in her life why this detached unemotionalism existed. What was their view of sex? The answers were similar. Sex is 'fun and games', 'a natural reaction', 'consenting adults and a good time'. 'Words like *love*, *share* and *happy* never entered the conversation.'

She decided to return to 'my celibate but happy style of life' and some time after making this decision, she talked to a close male friend who was airing complaints about the free-and-easy university sex circuit. In describing what he felt was the thinking of a majority of male students, he said,

Most of the times I found myself in bed with someone, I usually wished I had never gone that far. After I reached a point where I knew I would wind up spending the night with her, it was all downhill. I just went through the motions. There were times when all I wanted was to hurry up and get it over with. I finally stopped messing around when I realized sex is no good unless there is a true trust and love involved. Without it, it's just not worth the hassle.

Gretchen concluded her article with these words,

Now, with all this fuss about sexual freedom, it's a little hard to stand up and admit it's not what everyone imagines, especially to an anxious world that refuses to let the subject die. Consequently, here we sit, tight-lipped, and too embarrassed to say we couldn't find it. We can't admit it to the world and, worse yet, to ourselves.

Perhaps we could all begin to set the record straight—by saying that without love and trust, 'it's just not worth the hassle.'

Interesting, isn't it? Amid all the talk and practice of sexual freedom, liberation, and fulfilment, right here in the middle of the sexual revolution, we find a lot of casualties and phrases like 'a train that's been derailed', 'about as satisfying as a sneeze', 'as unemotional as a student card.' Could this be sex —the glorious, orgasmic, emotional experience worshipped by the masses? Something must have gone wrong. Could there be more to maximum sex than a rollicking game, 'a playful business', a succession of lovers and one-night stands, or marriages gone sour?

Perhaps love and trust are important. But on what basis? And where does sex fit in? Maybe sex is not the secret of loving.

Fortunately there is an answer, one as complete and realistic as it is positive and happy. It's time to consider the source.

# 3

# Who Thought up Sex?

For some time now, the law has required that all consumer products carry a label listing the ingredients they contain. Wouldn't it be great if sex had such a label—if there were a manufacturer's manual which explained how sex works and how we can get the most out of it?

Well, good news! There is such a manual. But you won't find it among the scores of sex-technique volumes bursting the shelves of your local bookshop. The most comprehensive information on sex and loving ever put into print originated 3500 years ago with a fellow named Moses. Writing by divine assignment from the 'Manufacturer', he set down the authoritative word about the origins and functions of sex. His book is called Genesis.

In the first two chapters he describes the process of original creation. And at the apex of that process, he writes, 'God created man in His own image... male and female He created them' (Genesis 1:27). There it is: sexuality has been a fundamental part of man from the very beginning—designed for man by God the Creator. There's no such thing as being human without being male or female.

A little later, in chapter two, we learn just how uniquely man and woman were made for each other. After labelling all the rest of his creative acts 'good', God said it was 'not good' for the man to be alone. And that's amazing. If anyone ever had the perfect environment, it was the first man—the ultimate example of God's creativity, living in God's perfect climate, walking with God himself in the cool of the evening, endowed with sufficient creativity to think up names for all the animals God had created. Yet something was missing. This man was still alone. He had the original built-in 'urge to merge'. And no amount of environmental perfection could diminish that.

So Moses tells us that God put Adam to sleep and fashioned a woman from one of his ribs. And for Adam it wasn't a side issue, either! In verse 23 Adam wakes up, sees the woman, and says, 'This is now bone of my bones, and flesh of my flesh.' A more up-to-date translation of the Hebrew would be a resounding 'Whoopee!...Where have you been all my life?'

Woman is the perfect complement to man. Man is the perfect complement to woman. They are designed in the creativity of God so that they are incomplete without each other. That's why Moses said, '...a man shall leave his father and his mother, and shall cleave to his wife; and *they shall become one flesh*' (verse 24, italics mine). In searching for the secret of sex, hang on to that one. Sexual expression is one of the key ways in which a man and a woman become 'one flesh'.

But what is so unique about woman that she is

indispensable to man? There are two ideas in the word Moses used: 'helper' and 'suitable'. The concept is that woman is fundamentally man's perfect match—the companion designed to provide for his wholeness, and he for hers. This basic fit was created to satisfy individual longings in such a way that when a man and a woman are united, they have the capacity to meet each other's basic psychological and emotional needs—to enable each other to become fully human according to God's original design.

If you're wondering whether the person you are going out with right now, or the man or woman with whom you're in love, is right for you, ask yourself, 'Do I have the desire and the capacity to meet his or her real needs? Is this person capable of more than merely satisfying my sexual urge, or raising my children, or bringing home the pay-packet? Do we seem uniquely made to complement each other?' The search isn't just for someone you can *live with*. Instead, the real search should be for someone you *can't live without*.

In this book's first chapter, I mentioned that Paul Lewis and I met while going out with twin sisters. I went out with Paula for more than two years while I was going to post-graduate college. As our relationship grew we became the best of friends. We enjoyed being with each other so much that falling in love was inevitable. Paula was an enormous encouragement to me. She supported me in my studies, she helped in my ministry, she shared my dreams and I shared hers. She had a wonderful sense of humour; she was attractive; she was everything I thought I had ever wanted in a wife. But, as the relationship continued and we talked about marriage, doubt began to creep into both our minds. The perfect peace that God gives when things are right was missing. Ultimately it became clear that we were not to marry each other. Breaking off that relationship was one of the most painful experiences of my life. But as perfect as the match was, Paula did not fill up my empty places in the way that Dottie, my wife, now does. Dottie is God's perfect complement for me. Paula wasn't.

It's interesting that Paul had a similar experience while he was at university. He went out with Carolyn for nearly four years. Everyone assumed they would get married. The match was a great one. They enjoyed the same interests, worked together in student government and leadership positions, had the same goals in life. Their relationship was happy and fun. But when it came time to consider the final commitment to marriage, something wasn't right. Paul had no peace from God. Carolyn wasn't able to fill up all his empty places in the way that Leslie now does. And I'm not referring to sex. I'm talking about the way personalities, gifts, intellectual and emotional needs merge to make a total twenty-four-hour-a-day relationship.

When Moses said, 'A man shall leave his father and his mother, and shall cleave to his wife; and they shall become one flesh,' he used the strongest Hebrew words possible to describe this 'leaving' and 'cleaving'. In leaving, the idea was to abandon and forsake the intimacy of the parent-child relationship, and to replace it with the intimacy of the husband-wife relationship. This new bond was to be as inseparable as the parent-child bond had been. Have you ever thought about how difficult it would be to become 'unborn' from your natural parents? This is

the concept behind the Hebrew word for 'cleaving'—
a separation-proof weld. And the evidence of that
union, the continual reminder, was to be sexual
intercourse, in which the man and woman become
'one flesh'.

Jesus affirmed this 1500 years later. He was in a
debate with the Jewish religious authorities, who
were testing him on the subject of divorce. They
were probing about the legal grounds on which a
man could divorce a woman. And Jesus, knowing
their motives, said, 'Have you not read... "the two
shall become one flesh"? Consequently they are no
more two, but one flesh. What therefore God has
joined together, let no man separate' (Matthew
19:4-6).

A little later the apostle Paul reinforced the principle in a letter to the people in the Christian church
at Corinth. He was upset about what some of the
deacons and elders were doing. Corinth was a city
filled with heathen temples. In fact, their worship
rituals probably made them one of the most 'religious'
cities in the world. In these temples, it was an act of
worship to have sexual intercourse with the temple
prostitutes. Paul was angry because some of the
Christian believers were reverting to their old ways
and tripping off to the temple to 'worship'. And it
wasn't to have a prayer meeting!

Paul wrote to them and said, '...do you not know
that the one who joins himself to a harlot is one body
with her? For he says, "The two will become one
flesh"' (1 Corinthians 6:16). They become one unit
in the same way that faith in Jesus Christ produces a
bond between God's Spirit and man's. In fact, God
often uses the marriage relationship as an analogy to

depict the union Christian believers have with him.

So what was in the mind of God the 'Manufacturer', the one who designed sexuality, the one who created the male and female sex organs, when he created the urges and passions which lead to the sexual union? In the mind of the originator of sex, the basic purpose was to create unity. Sexual intercourse is intended to be a demonstration of the unity between a man and a woman.

'But wait a minute,' you say. 'I thought the Bible taught that the primary purpose for sex was procreation—child-bearing. Isn't that right?' No! That's the myth uninformed critics of Christianity have propagated to serve their own ends. Child-bearing isn't the primary reason for sex. It's a secondary and very important reason, but it isn't the main reason God gave us sex.

The primary reason is the unity factor. It's to give a man and a woman 'one fleshness'—an experience in the physical realm which illustrates the intensity of the spiritual relationship a man or a woman has with God when he or she is reborn through Jesus Christ.

This unity in sexual intercourse provides for a man and a woman lasting enjoyment and the maximum fulfilment they can possibly know. That's why sex at the right time, with the right person, in the right relationship is so incredibly perfect! And that's why the abuse of sex ultimately produces such enormous disappointment.

A lot of people have missed the message of what sex is all about. They've never heard it because of the erroneous caricatures that have been drawn of the Christian view of sex. The Playboy philosophy, among many other voices, has led millions to believe that God is anti-sex and that the Bible is negative on sexual enjoyment and fulfilment. They've asserted that being a Christian believer means denying and repressing your sexual urges.

Nothing could be further from the truth. In fact, some of the most beautiful words ever written about love between a man and a woman are found in the Bible, in the Song of Solomon. Talk about two lovers, totally immersed in satisfying each other... the love-making poetry recorded there is incredible!

God isn't against sex. He's so *for* it that he wants every man and woman to understand how to get the most out of it. He wants them to realize it's not a casual toy; it's a fundamental pleasure to be carefully cherished, no matter how gratifying a 'quick fix' might seem.

Of course, a lot of stupid things have been said about sex in the name of Christianity. And when you put these mistaken images together, you can create a very sorry-looking caricature—a straw man. It may look like 'the Christian view of sex', but it's not even close. And when you destroy this 'straw man', as the Playboy philosophy has done, you really haven't destroyed anything. The facts are that sex is from God; he created it to fulfil and satisfy the deep urges he designed within every man and woman, and nothing will ever change these facts.

When we stop long enough in our quest for maximum sexual expression, we will begin to realize how foolish it is to try to write our own 'owner's manual'. Only the original designer really knows how to make the sexual experience the ultimately satisfying expression we want it to be. When we finally wake up to these truths, we'll find what we've been searching for. We'll discover the secret.

Now, a lot of people say to me, 'Come on, Josh, sex is just a physical act. Why, having intercourse is merely a physical thing, just the satisfying of a biological urge.' Well, let me tell you, that may be true of your neighbourhood tomcat. But because of the way God created it, sex for you and me involves all that we are. It's a complete sharing of ourselves, a complete vulnerability, a complete giving without holding anything back. That's what a maximum spiritual relationship with God is like. Sexual intercourse, being an illustration of that spiritual relationship, is like that too. Anything short of this complete sharing, no matter how pleasurable, is not the maximum sexual experience God created for you and me.

When I speak on this subject, I usually irritate a few people. I really annoyed one young chap on one occasion. He came to my hotel room, banged on the door, and as I opened it he pushed in and said, 'I didn't agree with some of the things you said tonight. What's wrong with a meaningful physical relationship with a girl?' (You know that phrase, 'a lasting, meaningful relationship'. One woman said, 'Yeah, I had four of them last month.')

So this chap said, 'What's wrong with a lasting meaningful relationship with a girl if you love her, if you don't want to hurt anybody, and if you just want to enjoy yourselves? Why, I've had intercourse with twenty-six women.' I said, 'Wow, what a capacity for love. Tell me, Dave, when you get married, do you want to marry a woman that's been one of the twenty-six meaningful relationships of another fellow?' He said, 'No.' Then I said, 'Dave, you're nothing but a hypocrite. That's how meaningful sex is to you. You don't want someone to take from the woman you marry the same thing you are taking from these other women.' You see, most fellows don't like used furniture, but they love to be in the antiquing business.

Sex, as it was created by God, is very meaningful. It's not something you 'get' or 'do' or 'have'. Sexual expression grows and develops as a result of the permanent, ongoing and maturing union between a man and a woman. It is evidence of the maximum oneness that God intended it to express.

Some people use this as an argument for premarital sex. They say, 'We'll have to have pre-marital sex to see if we're compatible.' Boy, you really would have to have a lot of it, because the problem of compatibility is not physical. The physical relationship nearly always works. The problem of compatibility is the problem of ultimate oneness—complementing each other in a way that makes for a giving and full personhood. And that involves the totality of who you are, your spiritual (God-sensitive) and soulish (man-sensitive) dimensions, as well as the physical dimension. In God's design, the more spiritual and soulish unity a couple has, the better their sex life will be, as it matures and develops over a period of time.

In one American university there's a Christian professor who is eighty-four years old. One day in a sociology seminar a woman student asked him, 'Tell me, sir, when do you stop enjoying sex?' He replied, 'I don't know, but it's some time after eighty-four.' And that's the way it was created to be. Sex is meant to be always growing, maturing, and developing into maximum unity and ultimate oneness.

This kind of unity, enjoyment and oneness can never be achieved by a 'one-night stand'. In fact, it can't really grow outside a marriage commitment that is final and permanent.

Sexuality originated in the creative act of God which put man on the face of this earth. You can choose not to believe this. You can decide instead that human sexuality is a mere biological function no different from the sexual attractions of two dogs running loose in the park. You can experiment and play all the mental and social games you want. But any other scheme or function for sexuality besides the one God had in mind is doomed to fall short of fulfilling the corresponding need and sexual longing God put within you. Sex is like any other process; it succeeds only when you follow the manufacturer's directions.

For all its apparent staying power and lasting attraction, sex is fragile. It takes time and needs security. It only really blossoms when enjoyed in the context of genuine unconditional love. In fact, you'll never discover ultimate sex until you have understood how to give and receive ultimate love.

It is often said that if you love someone, you'll express it sexually. The truth is that if you can't express your love apart from sex, it's not true love. So let's examine this true love. What is it like?

# 4

## *What's True Love Like?*

If you gave me only twelve minutes to speak to a psychology class on sexual fulfilment, I would talk about love. What you decide love is—the attitudes you have about it, how you express it, and how you respond to all the psychological games played in our society in the name of love—all of this determines whether you will ever find the sexual fulfilment you want. I believe that what my wife and I enjoy in our marriage is the result of what we both prepared for as single people.

A few years ago a lot of people called me prudish. They thought I was out of date. They said my ideas about sex and marriage were old-fashioned. But now many of them would give anything to reap what I'm harvesting from the attitudes to love I developed as a single person. The familiar saying is: 'You are what you have been becoming.' And nowhere is this more true than in the area of love and sex. The patterns of loving you practise now determine the quality of love you will experience later.

If you're feeling a bit confused about love, it's probably because you're unaware that there are really three kinds of love. As I describe them to you, I want you to use them as a mirror to evaluate the love relationships you now have with your friends, family and members of the opposite sex.

The first type of love is the only kind many people have ever known. It's what I call 'love *if*'. It's the love you and I give or receive when certain requirements are met. You have to do something to earn it. '*If* you are a good child, Daddy will love you.' '*If* you meet my expectations as a lover...*if* you satisfy my desires...*if* you go to bed with me, I will love you.' Parents often communicate this type of love by saying to their children, in effect, 'If you get good marks...if you choose a different set of friends...if you dress or act a certain way, you'll have our love.' The love is offered in exchange for something the lover wants. Its motivation is basically selfish. Its purpose is to gain something in exchange for love.

I've met so many women who know no other type of love than the one which says, 'I'll love you if you will perform.' What they don't realize is that the love they expect to win from someone by meeting his sexual demands is a cheap love which can't satisfy and which is never worth the price. This type of love is demonstrated by a student who said to me, 'Why should I want love when I can have sex? Love is surrender. Sex is conquest.'

'Love *if*' always has strings attached. As long as the conditions are met, things are fine. When there is resistance—against having sex, against getting an abortion—the love ceases to flow. Sadly, this kind of conditional love almost always destroys itself, because sooner or later one partner will fail to meet the requirements of the other.

Many marriages break up because they were built on this kind of love. The husband or wife turns out to be in love not with the actual personality of the partner, but rather with some imaginary, glorified, romanticized image. When disillusionment sets in, or the expectations cease to be met, 'love *if*' often turns into resentment. And tragically, the people involved may never know why.

The second type of love (and I think most people marry on the basis of this one) is 'love *because*'. In this love, the person is loved because of something he is, something he has, or something he does. In other words, the love is produced by a certain condition or quality in the loved one's life.

'Love *because*' often sounds like this: 'I love you because you're pretty'; 'I love you because you're rich'; 'I love you because you give me security'; 'I love you because you're so different from the others, so popular, so famous' etc. For example, you may know a woman who loves a particular man because he is a superb athlete. She just can't imagine herself settling for anything less than number one. It really doesn't matter much which particular fellow the athlete is. She isn't really in love with him; she's in love with his position, his status and his popularity.

Often someone will say to me, '"love *because*" sounds pretty good to me. I want to be loved for what I am, for the qualities and things in my life. What's wrong with that?' Nothing, perhaps. All of us want to be loved for something in our life. And it's certainly preferable to 'love *if*'. The 'if' kind of love has to be earned, and requires a lot of effort. Having someone love us because of what we are puts us more at ease. We know there is something about us which is lovable.

To be loved this way, however, soon becomes no better than trying to earn the 'if' kind of love. And it's a shaky foundation upon which to establish a marriage or any lasting relationship.

Consider, for example, the problem of competition What happens when someone comes along with more of the quality for which you are loved? Suppose you're a woman, and your beauty is one of the reasons for your husband's love. What happens when a more beautiful woman comes on the scene?

If the love of your girlfriend or wife is based on your salary, or the things and experiences it can buy, what happens if you lose your job, or become disabled, or for any other reason become unable to earn the salary you used to? Or what happens when someone with more money or more earning power comes on the scene? Will the competition put you on edge? Will it threaten your love? If it will, then yours is a 'love *because*' type of love.

There's another problem with 'because' love. It's due to the fact that most of us are two types of people. There's the person on the outside, the Josh McDowell or the Paul Lewis that meets the eye of the public. And then there's the other side of us, that deep-down-inside person that few, if any, really know. What I've learned from counselling people who have 'love *because*' relationships is that one or both partners are afraid to let the other know what they're really like deep down inside. They're fearful that if the truth were known they would be less accepted, less loved, or maybe rejected altogether.

Is there anything in your life that you cannot share with your partner out of fear of even minor discomfort or rejection? If so you'll have a difficult time experiencing maximum sex, because profound sexual intimacy requires 100% trust and giving. If there's any insecurity in your love, if there's any fear, the first place it will be manifested is between the sheets. This is because in a maximum and true sexual expression we become completely vulnerable—we're wide open to the other individual. It is this openness that makes possible maximum sexual gratification and sharing, and this same openness allows for the deepest sort of hurt if we're not completely accepted. In a 'love *because*' relationship you can never totally give of yourself in sharing physical love, because the risk of being hurt is so great.

I was sharing this with a student audience when one of the women listening burst into tears. She had been a beautiful woman, engaged to be married. One side of her face had become terribly scarred in a car accident. Plastic surgery had made repairs, but her relationship was a 'love *because*' relationship. When she was injured, fear entered her thinking, and the entire relationship deteriorated. It was a classic case of 'love *because*'. This attitude is reflected in the phrase, 'I love you, and I want you because...'. Much of the love in our lives is of this kind, leaving us very uncertain of its permanence.

Thankfully, there is yet another kind of love. A love so startling and so beautiful that I wish everyone could bend his will to accept it. It is love without conditions.

This love says, 'I love you in spite of what you may be like deep down inside. I love you no matter what could change about you. You can't do anything to turn off my love. *I love you—full stop!*'

'Love *full stop*' isn't a blind love. Far from it. It can

know a great deal about the other person. It can know the person's shortcomings. It knows the other's faults, yet it totally accepts that individual without demanding anything in return. There's no way you can earn this type of love. You can't do anything to increase it. You can't turn it off. It has no strings attached. It is different from 'because' love in that it isn't produced by some attractive quality in the person who is loved. This kind of love would love even the most worthless individual as if he were of infinite value.

'Love *full stop*' can only be exercised by a complete and fulfilled individual—one who doesn't have to keep taking from life's relationships to fill the voids in his or her own life. A fulfilled person is truly free to give in a relationship without demanding anything in return.

Whether you realize it or not, 'love *full stop*' is more important to you than anything else. If you are not at present experiencing this kind of love, you are probably still hoping that some day you will—or you are clinging to a treasured memory of a time in the past when you were. Life without something resembling this type of love will eventually lead to despair. 'Love *full stop*' is a giving relationship. It can't wait to *give*. The other two kinds of love can't wait to *get*. 'Love *full stop*' means freely giving yourself. And in this relationship there is no room for fear, frustration, pressure, envy, or jealousy.

When my wife and I became engaged, she wrote me a letter. In it she said, 'Darling, I know that you accept me just the way I am. I don't have to perform for you. I don't have to do or be any certain thing... you just love me'. And then she added, 'Do you know what that does for me? It causes in me a greater desire to be more of a woman for you.'

At this point a lot of fellows will say, 'Hey, if I loved my girl in spite of the way she looks, in spite of the way she does things, she'd just let herself go to pot.' No she wouldn't—because 'love *full stop*' is a giving love. It is actually God's love poured through an individual and it's so winsome, so irresistible, that it draws out the best in the other person. It causes creative changes in the other person. The changes aren't demanded, they are simply a natural response to unconditional love.

My wife loves me so much that I don't have to perform for her. Her unstoppable love triggers in me a natural desire to be the type of person she knows I ought to be. I don't have to be that way, I just want to. It's the natural response to her 'love *full stop*' for me.

This is what divine love is all about. God, speaking through the ancient prophet Jeremiah, says, 'I have loved you with an everlasting love; therefore I have drawn you with lovingkindness' (Jeremiah 31:3). You see, God loved me even when I didn't believe he had anything to say about my life. He loved me in spite of my sins. And the curious thing is that it triggered in me the natural response. I responded to his love. That's the real truth that led me to become a Christian.

I was speaking on sex, love and relationships at one university when a student from Germany stood up. He had the Kinsey Report in his hand. (Of course, it's a little out of date.) But he stood up and said, 'Look, McDowell, we want facts, not all this philosophizing about love. We want facts. The

Kinsey Report is factual and secular, and it recommends that girls have various pre-marital sexual experiences in order to be properly adjusted when they marry.'

Well, that sounded pretty good to most of the men in the room, and it deserved a straightforward response. I said, 'You may be right, but did you read why? In *Sexual Behaviour in the Human Female*, Dr Kinsey points out that it is common knowledge that many girls do not have pleasant sexual experiences the first few times. It often takes several weeks, months, or even a year to make the adjustments and to relax totally and enjoy sex completely. And then Dr Kinsey goes on to show the kind of love that many men have for their wives. He says the majority of men will not be patient with their wives in this area. Therefore he recommends that women have various pre-marital experiences with different men, because the man that supposedly loves her will not be patient with her.'

I can't think of a more depraved reason for doing something. I hope you women will do yourselves a favour and wait for that man to come along who loves you for who you are, with a giving love—the man who says, 'I love you *full stop*.' The man who won't rob you of the opportunity to express your love in marriage, but will be patient enough for you to make the necessary adjustments. There is no way in which a man can better demonstrate his love for his wife than by being patient and tender in the area of sexual adjustments.

Which of the three kinds of love would you like to have? Very few people purposely choose the 'if' kind of love. It requires a continual and endless effort to perform. Two other loves remain—and surprisingly, many people choose 'love *because*'. Perhaps it's more flattering to be loved this way. Being loved for something you are or have is satisfying. It builds your own opinion of yourself. But it is a fragile fabrication and ultimately self-defeating.

The secret of loving is the third type of love: 'love *full stop*.' It's not too common, because the only lasting source of this love is God himself. No individual can consistently display this kind of love without God's Holy Spirit living in him and controlling him. But God freely implants this love at the very centre of any individual who is willing to admit that he wants it, and that he needs God's help to love in this way.

Why is this love so scarce? Why is it such a secret? Because it runs cross-grain with man's pride. We don't like to admit that we can't be whatever we want to be through sheer willpower and determination alone. And we'd rather ignore this 'love *full stop*' because it requires discipline and self-control when it comes to sex. It requires that we let our emotions and physical urges know that they serve us; we do not serve them.

Are you tired of 'love *if*' and 'love *because*'? You can have 'love *full stop*'. It's the secret of loving. But if you want to begin experiencing it in your relationships with the opposite sex, it will probably involve some adjustment in your thinking. You'll need to re-educate your most important sexual organ.

# 5

## *Which Is Your Most Important Sexual Organ?*

When I speak on the Christian view of love and sex, it's not uncommon for one or two students to come up to me and say, 'Just a minute, having sex is a mere physical act. Why, it's no different from drinking a glass of water.' Well, let me tell you, there's a lot of difference between sex and drinking a glass of water. Whether exploitative or non-exploitative, sex involves all that you are as an individual. Sex is never merely a physical act. As we said earlier, the physical aspect of sex nearly always works. Any malfunction is usually in your mind. Your mind is your most important sexual organ!

I hope you're beginning to understand that sex was designed by God as a vehicle for enjoyment and for the expression of ultimate unity between a man and a woman within the bonds of a permanent and lasting relationship. I hope also that you're beginning to see casual sex can never be ultimately fulfilling or satisfying; that whatever gratification may be experienced on a one-night stand, or even in a series of longer relationships, only serves to dilute the possibility of sharing a truly robust and satisfying love. Yet all this is exactly opposite to what society is constantly telling us.

You and I are being continually bombarded by messages and pressures based on a sexual ethic and practice which is false and incomplete. When in the 1940s Kinsey questioned women about their sex lives, he found that a half to two thirds of married women reported having regular or frequent orgasms. Thirty years later, a survey of women revealed that three quarters of American women 'always or nearly always' had an orgasm during intercourse. The number of women achieving physical satisfaction has increased substantially. In view of this Jody Gaylin Heyward, writing in the May 1978 *Ladies Home Journal*, asks,

> Why, then, are women going to sexual dysfunction clinics in record numbers? And why are there so many stories of disappointment and disenchantment from therapists who are treating women of all ages? Maybe because there is more to being satisfied than mere physical pleasure. Maybe because frequency of orgasm doesn't measure psychological fulfilment.

Jody's right. Let's look at why sex is so often unfulfilling, even within marriage. It's because sex, as God created it, involves oneness on three levels; three different dimensions. If one of these three dimensions is missing, you are going to experience a diluted relationship.

The first dimension is obvious. It's the physical dimension. It's the one in which two people become one physically—a basic biological union.

The second dimension is the soulish dimension. In it the real you as a person, as a being with ideas, desires, and feelings, becomes one with another person.

The third dimension is the spiritual dimension, the one in which two people become one spiritually. Sex is a three-dimensional act, and if one of these three dimensions is missing you will experience a watered-down relationship and less than maximum fulfilment.

Most us us grow up unaware of these three crucial dimensions. We begin loving with the attitude, 'If I'm good at sex—if I can really please my partner physically—it doesn't matter what other problems we have. We'll be able to overcome them.' This is one of the biggest lies propagated today. A good sex life very seldom produces a good relationship. But I know one thing: a good marriage produces a fantastic sex life, because good sex is the result of a good relationship rather than the cause of it. Yet most people are striving to find real unity through physical love alone.

Let me give you an example of how some men think. A problem develops in their relationship with a woman, and the first thing they want to do is to go to bed. Why? Because they believe, 'If I can please my partner physically, the problem, no matter what it is, will take care of itself.' Usually, however, the woman doesn't want the man to touch her until the problem is talked out. Sex is the last thing she wants. That doesn't deter a lot of men, and they begin to pressure the woman until she gives in. As a result she develops negative attitudes towards sex.

This is why I stress the fact that unless you develop the spiritual and soulish dimensions of your lives, you're going to rob yourself and your partner in the area of your physical relationship.

How important, then, is the physical dimension? I think it's very important, but I believe in a maximum relationship. The physical dimension only makes up about one-twelfth of a marriage relationship. It's a great one-twelfth! However, it must be kept in perspective. That's why your mind is your most important sexual organ! I know many couples who have destroyed beautiful relationships because they have programmed false facts and attitudes about sex into their minds.

In preparing for this book, my wife and I gathered information from a number of reliable sources— people who constantly counsel and conduct research in the area of sex and marriage. Many of these sources point out that as much as 85-90% of problems that appear to be physical are really problems in the soulish and spiritual dimensions of life. Because the physical dimension is the most tangible part of a relationship, it's often the place where problems show up first.

When I say this, some people become critical and defensive. And it's these same people who tell me that sex is like 'a drink of water'. They come up after a lecture and say, 'Josh, not all sex is meaningful. With some people it is; with others it's not.' I think that attitude is totally in error. Every time you have a physical encounter, from heavy petting on, it's meaningful. It involves all that you are as an individual, including your mind.

And what is this problem with our minds? The difficulty is that many of us have been programmed incorrectly. We've been bombarded with misinformation. We've been told that the key to sexual fulfilment is to join the revolution, to cast off the old morality and enjoy the new, to experiment with a variety of partners, to move around and have our needs met. Discipline is out. Gratification is in.

It's like the familiar adage in computer talk: 'rubbish in, rubbish out.' If we've been programmed (or allowed ourselves to be programmed) with incorrect information, we're going to form incorrect conclusions. And that's what many of us have done. We have emphasized the physical instead of the mental. If we are to rediscover fulfilling love and satisfying sex, we have some re-programming to do.

I recently had the opportunity to interview a tremendous man, Dr Gerhard Dirks. He's one of the men who helped develop the computer. I've read that Einstein had an I.Q. of around 207; Dirks' is only 206! He has a brilliant mind, and he has held more patents for IBM than any other man alive. (You can read part of his exciting life story in Brandon Rimmer's book, *The Escapes of Gerhard Dirks*.)

During a four-and-a-half-hour conversation Dr Dirks shared with me how the computer was developed from the human body. It was thrilling. We talked about how the human body and mind are programmed. And I discovered that they are programmed in three ways: (1) visually (by what is seen); (2) audibly (by what is heard); and (3) mechanically (by what is done). I asked Dr Dirks to tell me specifically how the human body and mind are programmed in the area of sex. He shared his own convictions on the subject.

When a woman has intercourse with one man, he said, that man programmes her to respond visually, audibly, and mechanically to a certain set of actions.

Dr Dirks continued, 'I believe that what happens is this: a woman is programmed by one or two men—or twenty. Then she meets the man she marries, and she cannot totally respond to his programming because of the conflicting programming of prior experiences.' He added, 'I really believe that for optimum sex, it's best for two people to be programmed together.'

Dr Dirks then brought in the male perspective. When a man has a sexual experience, he never forgets it. It's programmed directly into his mind. Basically, women are programmed by touch and men are programmed by sight. While women are aroused or stimulated principally through touch, all a man has to do is see. A woman is turned on physically through caressing. All a man has to do is look—and *boom*, he's ready at 110% capacity!

This is why your mind is so important—the most important sexual organ you have. And how you programme your mind becomes critical. We men need to be especially careful of what we look at. Women need to be careful what they wear and how they are touched. And I realize that in the context of the society in which we live and love, what I'm saying borders on the absurd. But if the way in which you programme your mind directly affects your potential for sexual fulfilment, taking precautions is well worth the effort.

A lot of men and women are very casual about what they see or how they are touched. As a result, they numb the very sensory areas God created to arouse and fulfil them sexually. To express his attitude of freedom and liberation, a fellow may surround himself with pin-ups and lots of visual stimuli, and see sexually stimulating films. The long-term result will be a loss of sensitivity to the very things which God designed to fulfil him within the security of the marriage relationship. Because of this loss of sensitivity it will take more and more intense sexual stimulation to produce the same degree of arousal.

If a woman allows and encourages men to touch and fondle her in a casual manner, she too programmes herself for a diluted response to the man to whom she will one day want to give herself most completely.

In order to see the positive side of this programming principle, consider the effect on a man and woman within marriage. If a man's initial programming is with his wife, and hers with her husband, the first love-making encounter provides an initial burst of data and pleasure response in both of them. Those patterns of initiation and response are filed away in their minds. Their next sexual encounter adds to the programme and expands it further. The hundreds of subsequent experiences of life, interaction, and the physical sharing of love continue to build and further refine their mental programmes.

It's not hard to understand, then, why sex within marriage doesn't become boring, but rather more and more satisfying over an entire lifetime. When properly programmed, our minds are an incredible organ for sexual fulfilment.

For most of us, if we are to experience for ourselves maximum fulfilment in love and sexuality, we are going to need some rather dramatic and serious reprogramming. And I think I can speak confidently about this because I for one wasn't re-programmed until I was a student.

As a student I set out to destroy Christianity. I

thought it was a big farce and I wanted others to be as aware of this travesty as I was. But hard as I tried, I could not intellectually refute Christian truth. As a result of my intensive investigation, I came to the conclusion that Jesus Christ was who he claimed to be—the Son of God, the Messiah.

So in 1959, during my second year at university, I trusted Christ as my Saviour and Lord. I invited him to come into my life. And he began to change my mind and my thought forms. Within a year and a half he fulfilled me from the inside out. In fact, he so renewed and changed me that my sexual perspective changed. He made it possible for me to truly 'give' in a relationship without demanding something in return. That's when I learned the basic difference between 'love *if*' and 'love *because*' on the one hand, and 'I love you *full stop*' on the other.

I firmly believe that this is step one in the renewal of mind and life—letting Christ begin to remake you. And when you're in the process of renewal—when your life is under construction—you exert a little discipline in your approach to members of the opposite sex.

I get so tired of the lines I hear used on campus: 'If you love me, you'll let me,' or, 'But I can't help myself.' When you hear those or use them yourself, remember they mean strictly 'love *if*' or 'love *because*'.

Then, of course, there's the old standby, 'Everyone's doing it.' What a wishy–washy reason for doing something—just because someone else does it! I'm so glad that Jesus Christ gave me a new character and the capacity to avoid doing something for such a flimsy reason.

And finally there's the old standard, 'But just this

once?' I've seen so many long-standing 'just this once' relationships that I've lost count!

All of these 'lines' and motivations are based on a very cheap, conditional type of love. Renewal of the mind begins with Jesus Christ and continues as we exchange our lines and approaches for 'love *full stop*' relationships.

Whenever I begin to talk about mind renewal and Jesus Christ, someone will always say, 'Why all the fuss? Why should I wait for the right time and the right person? Why do you feel God wants sex to be reserved for marriage? What if you're in love and committed to each other but you just haven't gone through the formal procedure of a wedding ceremony?'

My answer is this: God designed sex and he has a lot to say about it. One of the things he says in the Bible is that we are to 'flee fornication'. Fornication is the biblical word for pre-marital sex. When I first heard this, before I became a Christian, I was irked. But the more I studied this instruction and the more I talked to young people and reflected on Scripture and personal experience, the more I became convinced that every time God gives a negative commandment in the Bible, there are two positive motives behind it. The first is for our protection. The second is for our private provision. In essence God was saying to me, 'Josh, wait. Because I love you so much, I'm going to protect you and provide for you so that you can have the best possible relationship with your wife-to-be.'

But why wait? I think one reason is to build self-control—something all of us need a little more of. There are many times *after* you're married when you

cannot have sex due to illness, separation, or some
stages of pregnancy. If you learn to control your sex
life before marriage, you can control it afterwards.
And this self-control adds the factor of trust to a
relationship.

If my wife knows that I was able to control my sex
life before marriage, it builds trust in her mind and
strengthens our relationship when I'm on the road
travelling. You say, 'Oh, that's childish.' Perhaps it
is, but it gives us and our marriage an advantage.
Because of the way God designed sex, it requires a
total abandonment of yourself to the other person.
And that requires 100% trust. When there's distrust
in a relationship, you're in trouble. Discipline before
marriage makes possible maximum love and sex later.

A lot of people say, 'I want to wait for the right
time and right relationship for sex. But how can I?'
Others add, 'I haven't waited in my physical relationship, but from now on I want to wait. How do I
explain this to my boyfriend when we've been having
sex?'

I'm the first to admit that stopping after you've
started is a real problem. It's just plain tough to give
it up. But I think it's necessary to do so. And while
my answer to these questions is simple, it's not easy. I
suggest that you tell your lover a simple, direct 'no',
and explain your reasons. If he (or she) persists, he or
she doesn't really love you. What was represented as
love was really only a desire for sexual release. I don't
care if it's a man pushing a woman's standard in this
area, or a woman pushing a man's; I believe that
anyone who seeks to compromise you in one area can
attempt to compromise your standards or desires in
other areas. The area may be lying, cheating, or

whatever; this type of individual is not good marriage material. I wouldn't want someone with a compromising approach to be the mother of my children.

If you want to programme your mind positively, I'll give you some practical ideas. In addition to the essential basis, a vital relationship with Jesus Christ, and being careful of the 'lines' you use or respond to, here are other steps you can take.

Over 2700 years ago the writer of Proverbs wrote of man, 'as he thinks within himself, so he is' (Proverbs 23:7). (And by the way, that applies to women too.) The point is: what you think about determines who you are. Thoughts .... attitudes .... actions .... accomplishments is the sequence. And 750 years later Paul, under God's inspiration, added these words, 'Do not be conformed to this world, but be transformed by the *renewing of your mind*' (Romans 12:2). The principle, then, is: what you think, you become. The way to change your actions is to renew your mind.

I mentioned earlier the computer phrase, 'rubbish in, rubbish out.' Let's be specific. Watch what you *read*. You know what's good for you and what's not. If there's a certain magazine or book that causes you to fantasize erotically, it would be best to leave that book or magazine alone. Erotic fantasies can cause unrealistic expectations which may never be fulfilled later in marriage.

If you find the *films* you're seeing are slowly (or quickly) eroding your new-found convictions, you may have to stop seeing them. Don't be stupid; discover what affects you. You have to make the decision. I can't give you iron-clad standards that will satisfy all your requirements. But I can say, 'As a person thinks, so is he.' And I can unequivocally say that we all need to be transformed by the renewal of our minds through Jesus Christ.

Another crucial area for renewal is your *speech*. What you do is affected almost as much by what you say as by what you think. If you are constantly involved with off-colour jokes, sexual innuendoes, and provocative talk, it's going to influence you and those around you. I'm certainly not saying it's wrong to talk about sex, but be careful of the context. Are you simply rephrasing society's view that sex is a game—a 'playful business'? Or is your talk reinforcing the beauty, importance and values of a harmonious personal relationship?

And finally, be careful what you do when you go out with someone. Once you've crossed a certain point physically, it's hard to return. So decide in advance how much sexual stimulation you and your partner will give one another. And beware of the setting. Regardless how 'renewed' your mind is, sitting in the back of a car listening to music at 2 a.m. is plain stupidity if you're serious about the sanctity of sex.

But 'no-no's' are only half the answer. You need to refill the areas of your mind you've emptied. Renewal involves re-programming.

The psalmist had a suggestion that holds true today: 'How can a young man keep his way pure? By keeping it according to Thy Word' (Psalm 119:9) I'm a firm believer in the importance of Bible study Feeding on God's word will counteract all the pro gramming you get from the world's system. (I sugges that if you haven't done much Bible reading before you find a modern translation of Scripture and begin to read. Start in the gospel of John in the New Testament; later read the Old Testament.) You'll find that as you respond obediently to God's word, your life will take on unbelievable meaning and some of the emptiness you formerly tried to fill with sexual activity will be filled with God's own love for you. That's mind renewal. And after all, your mind is your most important sex organ.

# 6

## Can I Have A Fresh Start?

By this point, you've probably formed one of three opinions concerning what I've said about sex and loving. You're either saying, 'Josh, you're absolutely right. I agree and I've been trying to live and love the way you have described.' Or you are saying, 'You're out of your mind—a reject from the nineteenth century. I'm going to live the way twentieth-century people do.'

Still others of you are saying, 'It's pretty new to me, but the message makes sense. My lifestyle doesn't even come close to what you have described. At times I've felt a bit uneasy about some of my sexual patterns; sometimes I've felt like a loser. Now I feel downright guilty. I want to make a new start. I want to clean up my whole sex life. I'd like to have 'love *full stop*' but I don't know where the change should start.'

Since those of you in the first category already understand the secret of loving, and you who are in the second category aren't interested, I'd like to talk for a moment to everyone who has responded in the third way. Let me say at the outset that there is enormous hope. You *can* change and have the kind of life you want. Here's how.

Some of you in this group are not Christian believers. I'll address you first. And then I want to talk to you who are Christians but still find yourself a long way from the mark. I've met hundreds, and heard from thousands of you who have deep guilt about your sexual behaviour.

If you are one who does not yet have a personal relationship with Jesus Christ, the answer to your guilt feelings is not a long list of sexual taboos. Nor is the solution found in saying, 'Free sex for you is fine.' I think the real starting point for you and everyone else is where it was for me in 1959—the discovery of Jesus Christ. That's right, an exciting life-changing encounter with Jesus Christ. Before you tune me out, let me give you two basic reasons why.

First is the area of forgiveness—the cleansing of the conscience. I believe one of the first steps towards control in the area of sex (or any area, for that matter) is the experience of forgiveness and the removal of guilt. God is in the forgiving business. One of the major reasons Jesus came to the earth was to forgive men and cleanse their consciences. That's why the Bible says, 'Though your sins are as scarlet, they will be as white as snow' (Isaiah 1:18). That's the primary reason Jesus Christ died on the cross—to forgive you, to forgive me, to forgive us. We are all in need of forgiveness.

The director of one mental institution said that 50% of his patients could go home if they knew they were forgiven. When Billy Graham was lecturing in Honolulu a group of psychologists was sent there to criticize his talk. They could only agree unanimously on one point: when Dr Graham called for people to

repent and receive God's forgiveness through Christ
it was a psychologically sound move because people
needed to be forgiven.

Do you know why people feel guilty? Because they
*are* guilty. The Bible points out that all of us have
sinned and fallen short of God's glory. 'All' includes
you and me. But if you come to Jesus right now and
ask him to become your Lord and Saviour (giving
him authority to direct your life), he will immediately
forgive you and cleanse your conscience.

When I told one student this he replied, 'How do
you know God will forgive me? You don't even know
what I've done.' I said, 'I don't care what you've
done, I don't care how awful you've been. God loves
you and he will forgive you and wipe the slate clean.'

How can I know this? What gives me this
confidence? First, it's written down in God's book,
the Bible. And God doesn't lie. For an enormous
number of reasons, I have confidence in his word.
Second, I distinctly remember that night when I
confessed Christ as Saviour; when I went to bed I
slept like a baby. And not once since then has guilt
ever kept me awake.

The second reason why I think it's important that
you turn to Christ is the whole area of freedom. Real
freedom. Jesus Christ has the power to set us free.
You see, the Christian life is a supernatural life.
According to Scripture, and according to my
experiences and those of millions of other Christians
throughout history, when someone trusts Christ, the
Holy Spirit enters into his life in a supernatural way
and begins to change him from the inside out. He is
literally 'under construction'.

This freedom that Christ gives is completely

different from the world's idea of freedom. The world tells us we're free in sex through indulgence. Jesus makes a lot more sense. He says, 'You're free in sex through control.' With Christ, we *can* control this area of our lives. And until we can control it, we're never really free. We're in bondage to our passions.

The reason so many people espouse free sex is that they seemingly have no other choice. They can't control themselves. But if you come to Christ and confess him as Saviour and Lord, he'll forgive you, cleanse you, enter into your life, and change you on the inside in much the same way that he changed me. He will give you the capacity to say no in areas of your life in which you need to say no, and yes in areas where you need to say yes.

I've described this dynamic relationship with Jesus Christ, but I haven't really told you how to begin such a relationship with him. You might be saying, 'I didn't know that Christianity was a relationship with Jesus Christ. I'd like to know Christ personally. I'd like to know that I'm forgiven, that my conscience is cleansed. I'd like to know for sure that Jesus Christ lives in me.'

I remember when I had that attitude and didn't know what to do. A friend of mine said to me, 'I'll pray the prayer that I prayed to trust Christ and maybe my words will help you to express to God your desire to trust him.' And ever since Jerry did that for me, I've been so appreciative that I've wanted to do it for other people. So I'll share with you what Jerry shared with me. If you want to pray it where you are right now, I encourage you to do so. And as you pray, remember that God says in John 1:12, 'But as many as received Him, to them He gave the right to become children of God.'

This is the prayer that I prayed:

> Lord Jesus, I need you. Forgive me and cleanse me.
> Right this moment I trust you as Saviour and Lord.
> Take over the throne of my life; change me from the
> inside out. Thank you that I can trust you. In Christ's
> name, Amen.

It's not the most complicated prayer you've ever
heard—but it *is* the most significant. With that
prayer, you can begin a permanent new relationship
with God.

If you just prayed that prayer, I'd like to suggest
that you read the third chapter of the book of John
three times before you go to bed tonight. Before you
read it, pray a prayer something like this; 'God, if you
are God and Christ is your Son; if what I read in this
book is true and you really did come into my life in
response to the request I just made, and you forgave
me; then please give me the conviction of it. Help me
to know internally that it's true.' Then read John
chapter 3 three times. In the following days and
months, look for changes in your life in two areas—
attitudes and actions.

When a fundamental change has occurred at the
very centre of your being, it's only natural that it will
begin to show in various ways. Often there is a rather
immediate sense of new inner peace—that insecure
feeling is replaced with a sense of calm security.
You'll find yourself beginning to respond to life's
circumstances in new ways. Things that used to
frighten or anger you may no longer do so. You will
begin to express a more selfless love than you've ever
had before.

There may be other changes in attitude or actions which will be uniquely given by God to you. To gain insight and understanding of your new life read the rest of John in your Bible, and look for a group of Christians with whom you can communicate and learn more about your new faith.

Now let me address myself to Christians—you who have previously invited Christ into your lives. Strange as it may seem, Chirstians can have more problems in the area of sexual control than non-Christians. As I've said before, sex involves the physical, soulish, and spiritual parts of us. Therefore, when a Christian man and woman enter into a close personal relationship, they begin with a common spiritual bond. And if their personalities integrate easily, there will be a natural tendency to progress into the physical area. Unless they realize this, control can be very difficult.

Charlie Shedd, who has often written on this subject, facetiously says, 'I wouldn't encourage unmarried couples to pray together. Good prayer leads to good sex.' And he's right—with the right person, in the right situation (marriage), sex is good and lovely. And so is prayer. I'm a firm believer in the truth that the stronger your spiritual bond is, the stronger your sexual bond can be.

Several months ago a national magazine did a survey of religious men and women and concluded that 'religious conviction adds to sexual enjoyment'. They discovered that where there were strong religious convictions, there was a greater enjoyment sexually. I think the primary reason for this parallel between religious conviction and enjoyable sex is Jesus' teaching that people are of value. You don't use people. You think first of what you can *give to* them rather than what you can *get from* them. In marriage this attitude of giving rather than getting eliminates many sexual problems. Before marriage it can lead to a few problems however, because 'love *full stop*' is so winsome that people naturally gravitate towards greater physical involvement.

If you are a Christian and have failed in the area of sexual control and feel guilty, let me tell you how to lose that guilt for ever.

Step one is confession. Forgiveness is as important for a Christian as for a non-Christian. When Jesus Christ died on that cross almost 2,000 years ago, he died for every sin you ever committed or ever will commit—past, present, or future. You may say, 'Wait a minute, what about my future sins?' Well, 2,000 years ago all your sins were future—but Christ died for you.

'If my sins have been forgiven,' you may ask, 'why should I confess them?' I think there are two reasons. One, the Bible tells us to. The apostle John, writing to Christians, says, 'If we confess our sins, He is faithful and righteous to forgive us our sins and to cleanse us from all unrighteousness' (1 John 1:9).

The second reason is personal and pragmatic. I encourage believers to confess so they can start experiencing what they already have—forgiveness. So many Christians run around as if they've been put on parole, when in reality they've been pardoned. And they don't realize the difference between the two. When you're on parole you go to see your parole officer regularly. The crime is still on record. You have a list of restrictions for your life. You live under constraint, constantly on guard, wondering if you're doing something wrong. When you're pardoned you're totally free. No restrictions. No parole officer. It's as if the crime had not been committed.

For an even better understanding of pardon, let's look at the Greek word for 'confession'. The Bible was written in Greek and Hebrew, and for a more complete understanding it's often important to discover what the original words really meant. The Greek word for 'confession' is made up of two root words, one meaning 'the same' and the other meaning 'to say'. Thus, confession means to 'say the same thing as God says' about sin. And what does God say? He says: (1) sin is wrong; (2) sin is forgiven. When we confess our sins the Holy Spirit applies the forgiveness that has already been earned by Christ at the cross, and we start experiencing it.

The first thing I urge Christians who have problems with sex to do is to confess their sins to God. The second thing I encourage them to do is to put Jesus Christ at the centre of their sex lives. What does that mean?

First, Jesus Christ is more concerned about your sex life than you are. I know some of you will find this hard to believe but it's true, and it means that you can trust him completely. Putting Christ at the centre means trusting Jesus Christ in every area of your life. It means allowing the Holy Spirit, the source of your strength, to give you the power to say no and to control your life. It means allowing God to direct you in cultivating the Christian sexual mind as we described in chapter 5. And when the Spirit does, you'll find sexual success before marriage (in control) and after marriage (in freedom).

Up to this point I've talked individually to those of

you who are non-Christians and then to you who are Christians. Now I'd like to speak about forgiveness in more detail. Many counsellors I know feel that the number one hang-up in the areas of self-acceptance, self-concept, and relationships with others is lack of forgiveness. Forgiveness operates on three levels: God, self, and others. We have already talked about forgiveness from God. He promised to forgive us. Jesus Christ paid the price for our sins; forgiveness is settled and we can experience it. God says it and I believe it, because I've read it, heard it and personally experienced it. That's level one.

The second level is self. Many people have a hard time forgiving themselves. They feel they've botched life so badly that no one can forgive them. Let's examine this attitude. If the Creator of the universe says you're forgiven, if he has wiped the record clean, then you are forgiven. God forgives you. Do yourself a favour: forgive yourself. God still loves you. He still accepts you. He says you're forgiven.

If it will help, write out the statement, 'I am forgiven by God and I forgive myself. God has given me a new clean life. He loves me and I love myself.' Then say the statement aloud. What you read, hear, and say can and does affect you. Writing, reading and speaking forgiveness may provide the impetus you need to accept it. If you like, look for yourself at a few of the scriptures on this subject. Read Psalm 103:12; Isaiah 43:35; Hebrews 10:16-18; I John 1:9; 2:1-2.

Level three concerns others. On this level there are two parts. One is the forgiveness of others—those who may have hurt or abused you in love, sex, or in other ways. We have not only the authority but also the responsibility to forgive. The Lord's Prayer says:

'forgive us our debts, as we also have forgiven our debtors' (Matthew 6:12). Do you know what you are saying when you say those words? You're asking God to be as gracious and loving and forgiving with you as you are gracious, loving and forgiving with others. If after our prayers we go out with an unforgiving heart towards others, it's spiritual hypocrisy.

In the gospel of Matthew Christ talks about forgiveness. When Peter asks how many times he should forgive someone, Jesus says, 'not seven times, but up to seventy times seven' (Matthew 18:22). The resulting figure of 490 is not important; it's the principle of the thing. Forgive a person until you have lost count.

An unforgiving heart causes bitterness. The longer you are unforgiving, the longer this 'root of bitterness' will grow in you until finally it consumes you. And that will destroy you as well as your relationship with those around you.

I'm sure that some of you have been deeply hurt by others who have not even bothered to come and ask your forgiveness. God wants you to forgive them anyway. Nowhere in Scripture does it say, 'Only forgive them if they come to you; otherwise don't forgive them at all.' At this point your forgiveness benefits you more than it does them. It clears the decks in your life so you can get on with the business of living and loving. It frees you from bitterness to partake of God's abundant life.

The second part of forgiveness with others is receiving forgiveness. Jesus taught that if you have something against your brother or sister, you are to drop what you're doing and make it right. If we have wronged a person, I believe that in most cases it's important to ask forgiveness and then to accept it. I say 'most cases' because I think there are some instances in which asking forgiveness may open old wounds. Like going to a former girlfriend whom you haven't seen for twelve years and who is happily married, and bringing up an unpleasant memory that she may never have shared with her husband. I think you and the Holy Spirit need to make the decisions in those areas.

Forgiveness is important. Forgiveness is biblical. Some of the great personalities in Scripture were people in desperate need of forgiveness. David, called by God a man after his own heart, committed adultery with Bathsheba and then had her husband killed in battle so he could marry her. David's confession of his sin to God is recorded in the beautiful Psalm 51. God forgave him and continued to use and bless him.

The apostle Peter denied Christ three times at a crucial moment in history. Yet God forgave him and made him an integral part of the early church. The apostle Paul was responsible for the deaths of hundreds of believers before his conversion. But God forgave him. And these are only three of the many instances recorded in Scripture. God is in the business of forgiving, and we need to accept his love and grace.

Granted, there may be some consequences of our sin remaining even though we are forgiven. If you were responsible for a woman becoming pregnant and she gave the baby up for adoption, you'll always know that a child of yours exists somewhere. If you lost your virginity so long ago you can't remember when, some of those memories will linger. But Christ has an amazing way of healing even memories so that the consequences of past sins will not immobilize you.

A friend of mine who also works with students says that if you have lost your virginity you can get it back again. That's right, you can have it back again. Obviously you can't reclaim it physiologically or historically, but spiritually and psychologically you can. For God says in his word that when he forgives you your sin, he forgets it. God buries it in the deepest sea, and to him you are chaste again. Because of that, you don't have to continue to carry your grief over sexual sins. You are free to move forward as a new person. God has forgiven and forgotten.

That's another great characteristic of God. Not only does he forgive, he forgets! He wipes your slate clean. You can feel fresh and new and clean, regardless how sordid your past. Your new-found good intentions can become a reality because of Christ's love and the unmerited favour he sends your way. Getting a fresh start is usually only a dream. Through confession and Christ's sacrifice on the cross, it can be your reality.

Now that you have a fresh start, let's talk about where to go from there. In the next three chapters, let's take a look at pre-marital and marital relationships.

# 7

## *Do Men Respond Differently From Women?*

Do you remember the first time you went out with a member of the opposite sex? I do. I was so excited I started taking a bath at 4:30 p.m. I got my sister's bubblebath, flooded the tub, and literally scrubbed myself everywhere! Tying a tie was a major effort. I had to give myself half an hour for that event. I tied the thing seven times to make sure it hung perfectly. And then my hair! Every hair had to be just right. I got my sister's mirror, held it carefully behind my head, and searched for stray hairs that needed to be plastered down with a little more cream.

And then the cologne—was that important! The first time I used it I had no idea how much to put on. I have an older brother who used to buy expensive colognes, and on this particular occasion I sneaked into his room with the attitude 'if a little is good, a whole lot is better' and I went to work with a variety of his bottles. I smelled like a cologne factory by the time I left the house.

As I walked from my house to the girl's I was so nervous that I thought I was going to throw up in the nearest bush. The path to her door looked so big and so long, and I was so scared, that I walked round the block one more time before taking the hike up it! I remember going to the door and ringing the bell. There I was—almost drowned in cologne, feeling really ill and hoping no one would answer. But someone did—her dad. 'Hi, I'm Josh,' I said meekly. 'Come on in,' he answered. I think he may have been as nervous as I was (it was also his daughter's first time out), but he didn't show it. 'Thank you, sir,' I said. And there we sat in deep silence punctuated by short questions and shorter answers.

'How's school going, son?'

'Very well, sir.'

'How's the football team doing?'

'Hmm, not so well, sir.'

'How's your dad doing?'

'Very well, sir.'

And then she came in. She was next to the most beautiful woman I'd ever seen. She must have started getting ready at 3:30!

We walked to the local cinema. It wasn't the most enjoyable evening I'd ever had because I was so nervous, but I was proud as I opened my wallet with my ten crisp notes (I got a ten-month advance on my allowance) and held it, à la Rockefeller, as though it contained the total value of the Mint.

Sitting in the cinema was uncomfortable. I didn't know whether you talked to your girl during the film or not. I started to sweat profusely. I whispered into her nose, thinking it was her ear. It was a memorable evening.

But as we all know, after the first date you get more experienced and more forward. All week long you think about holding her hand. And the next time you go over to her house, you call her dad 'George' instead of 'sir'. The next time you go to the cinema, you plan your big move. You slide back in the seat, brace your left foot, raise your right shoulder and rather nonchalantly slip your right arm round her shoulder. And you sit there in that terribly uncomfortable position trying to watch the film. Ten minutes later the shoulder pains begin, starting at the top of your shoulder and slowly moving down your arm until you think you'll die before the film ends.

As time moves along, the high of 'putting your arm round her shoulder' begins to wear off and you have to move to other things. Progress continues....

All of us have such memories. I've told them from the male perspective, but I'm sure you women have your own stories and your own feelings. Regardless of who you went out with or where you went there is one similarity—physical progression. And that progression involves what I call the Law of Diminishing Returns. One kind of physical contact satisfies for a while and then it starts to wear off. Then you have to have a little more and that starts to wear off. Then a little more and a little more. You go a little further and a little further still, and before you know it you've gone too far.

It's natural to go out with people. And because of God-given feelings we have for touching and caring, also natural to want to reach out and touch that other person. But there are dangers in touching. And as individuals desiring God's best for our lives, we need to be aware of this desire for physical progression and the Law of Diminishing Returns.

Whenever I talk about progression and diminishing returns, people always ask, 'How far is too far?

How far can we go? How much can we get? Can I
touch the knuckles, the wrist, the elbow? Can I go as
far as the shoulders, as far as the...? How far can I
go?'

Many people want me to give them a standard.
But giving everyone a standard would be one of the
worst things I could do. Some people would go right
out, skip all the preliminaries, go immediately to the
furthest reaches of the standard I'd set, and then
work out ways they could break it. That's how many
of us are.

By now, I'm sure you know I believe everyone
ought to have a standard. And I think most of you
can guess what my standard is. If not, check out the
New Testament. But what the issue finally boils
down to is a question of the will. What do you really
want out of love and life and sex and marriage? That
will determine how far you go and what you do. And
once you set your standard, you need to be keenly
aware of two things. One, remember that once you
do something two or three times, it's pretty hard to
stop. Once you get that motor running, it's hard to
turn it off. Remember the Law of Diminishing
Returns. What turned you on a month ago will seem
pretty tame tonight.

Your most important sexual organ—your mind—
has to be involved if you're going to succeed in male-
female relationships. And by 'succeed', I definitely
don't mean 'score'. I mean to feel good about the
relationship: to have an absence of guilt and a good
positive feeling about your partner, yourself, God,
and your future.

It means sitting down beforehand in a non-sexual
environment and deciding what marriage means to

you. It means loo

foreplay, which is t

mate encounter—p.

planning the evening

up in a compromising

rather not be. It also m

and the opposite sex. As y

so will your standards.

In chapter 5 we talked a

differences between a man an

some of those conclusions. On

what turns them on. As Dr Gerh            said to me,

'Women are basically programn       d by touch, and

men by their eyesight.' As a friend of mine says,

'Breasts are the sex symbols of femininity in our

world. So, a girl who is well-endowed, wearing a

T-shirt that says, 'Pinch me, I'm real,' makes it very

difficult for a man to keep his cool.' However, women

don't have to be well-endowed or wear message T-

shirts to turn a man on.

I think most women know what's provocative and

what's not. They know that how they look helps to

turn a man on. And because of this, I suggest that

women think seriously about what they wear. What

they choose when going out sends off all kinds of

signals.

If a man is trying to keep a relationship from

becoming too physical, he needs to be alert to what

he's doing with his hands. I'm not advocating a total

hands-off policy. But remember, touch is what turns

a girl on, and if you want to be responsible you need

to exercise caution in this area.

Another difference is in the area of sex and love.

From my conversations with men and women, I'm

more dominant in the mind of
more paramount in the mind of a

give you an example from marriage. Let's
husband is at work and sees a woman in a
ght jumper. Boom . . . . all he can think about is *s-e-x*.
He goes to coffee break sex, lunch break sex, all he
can think about is getting home.

He drives home through a sex light and charges
into the house where he discovers his wife has had a
bad day. She drove the car through the garage,
burned a hole in his shirt, dropped a dozen eggs, and
has a headache that not even a television advert can
cure. The last thing on her mind is sex. And unless
the husband is patient and tender and takes the time
to slowly bring his wife to his intensity, tension will
develop. By the way, that's why learning self-control
before marriage pays off after marriage.

Now let's put the wife in a similar situation. She's
at work and sees a man in a tight jumper and it may
do nothing for her. But perhaps during the day she
remembers a loving touch from her husband and as
she dwells on that, she begins to think about love,
*l-o-v-e*. She goes to coffee break love, typewriter love.
She jumps into her car and drives home, only to
discover that her husband has had a bad day. He
dropped cake mixture all over his newly-waxed floor,
burned a hole in her skirt while ironing, and in a fit of
frustration has ripped the handle off the fridge door.
The television doesn't work and he can't watch his
favourite soap opera. The last thing on his mind is
sex. But with loving words and tender caresses the
wife says, 'Darling, how are you?' . . . and he's ready!

Believe it or not, my preposterous illustration

communicates two truths: the seeing-male, touching-female emphasis and the whole area of timing. Men seem to have the ability to get charged up quickly. A woman's sexual interest and energy builds more slowly.

This is important from two standpoints. Women should understand the nature of men, realizing that the man may experience high sexual feelings before the woman does. What may seem purely innocent to the girl may be charging up the fellow. And I think men need to realize that a woman can be turned on through touch and kind words. What might seem innocent to you—some sweet words of love that you read in a novel, and a soft touch—may be arousing her more than you intended.

In summary, let me say that the sex drive is good, created by God to enable a man and a woman to experiece an unparalleled relationship based on mutual trust, love and commitment. But when sex is handled irresponsibly, problems arise. It is my prayer that with an understanding of the process of progression, the Law of Diminishing Returns and the sexual differences between a man and a woman, you can control rather than be controlled by this God-given gift.

# 8

## *What Makes Relationships Fun*

Think back for a moment to the times in your life which you remember as being the best, happiest, most satisfying and most carefree. I'll bet most of them are times when you were involved with other people, even older adults, in laughing, listening, and just plain kidding around. These fun times weren't exactly your typical date but, really, that's the point. If a relationship is to be fun and free, sensual ploys and 'games' can't be the main focus. A memorable and happy date is one on which both people are able to freely be themselves.

The constant feedback I get from men and women in my mailbox and in personal conversation reveals that most relationships miss this objective by a mile. Sensual ploys and sexual gamesmanship—exploitation in the name of love—is the rule rather than the exception. No wonder so many people experience so much heartache. Going out is supposed to be fun, and it can be if you understand its purposes and set some goals for yourself.

One of the first things a man or woman must do is to think through his or her purpose in going out. Of course, responding to the basic attraction of a person of the opposite sex is a fundamental reason for a relationship. But there are a lot of fellows and girls who really aren't ready to go out, because they haven't thought seriously about it—what it is for and what they want it to be in their lives.

You may say, 'Come on, everybody goes out. It's only the normal, natural thing to do.' That's true, but beyond the mere response to intense peer-group pressure, why have a boyfriend or girlfriend?

One of the first purposes is socialization. As we mature, our skills in interpersonal relationships, conversation and understanding need to grow up with us. Going out is a terrific way to learn more about yourself, to become skilled at sensing the needs and feelings of another person, and to learn how to turn that insight into responsive action. Good relationships prepare you for a happy, growing and lasting marriage. Poor habits from earlier relationships breed the fragile and short-lived marriages with which we're all too familiar.

Of course, the second key purpose for going out is the selection of a life partner. One thing is rather obvious: the person you marry will be one of the people you went out with. The typical progression is from casual meetings to doing things as friends to a steady relationship to engagement to marriage. It rarely happens any other way. Earlier relationships serve to cultivate and sharpen your tastes, and improve your ability to recognize the character and personality qualities which best mesh with your own. It's a chance to see if the kind of person you *think* you'd like to spend the rest of your life with really *is* the kind of person you'd like to spend the rest of your life with.

At this point in your understanding of the secret of loving, it should be quite obvious that the focus of going out is not sexual exploration, technique development, or conquest. Nothing short-circuits a growing friendship and quality communication like premature physical involvement. John White points out in *Eros Defiled* that 'premarital sexual excitement too often becomes all-important, as many unmarried couples have discovered. It blocks the very communication it is designed to promote.'

'Why?' you ask. Because that's the way God, the 'Manufacturer', created man. When God fashioned man in his own image, he built within him a primary need for divine interaction and fellowship. To make this possible, he created at the very centre of man a spiritual capacity, an ability and drive in the spiritual realm every bit as potent and natural as man's sexual drive in the physical realm. This spiritual ability is unique to man. No other creature on earth has this same urge and capacity.

The reason we sometimes fail to recognize the importance of this spiritual capacity is that, in our arrogance, we've chosen to ignore God and his principles and to put our own desires and will in God's place. The result is always profound separation and alienation. The 'spiritual light' at the centre of our being goes out, and we're left groping for the essence of life. The religious quests and longings which fill the pages of human history testify to the reality of this incredible loss.

It only stands to reason, then, that if a man and a woman wish to experience a maximum oneness, it will have to include mutual and intimate communion on the spiritual level. That's one of the goals of marriage. And since going out is a process that prepares us for marriage, it becomes a priority goal in that relationship as well. Without spiritual oneness, there can never be complete sexual oneness and fulfilment. Sexual intercourse was designed by God to be an outward expression of this inward reality between two people.

The second area of union between a man and a woman is on the soulish level. We've mentioned this before. It's the coming together of personalities. It's the interface of attitudes, values, goals, likes, dislikes, idiosyncrasies—all the facets that make you fun, likable, and uniquely you. Many of the 'love *because*' qualities people see in each other exist on this soulish level, and those undesirable negative qualities hidden away in each of us reside here also. These are the personal liabilities which are only overcome by 'love *full stop*'.

The going out stage, leading up to engagement, is the optimum time during which soulish oneness can begin to develop alongside spiritual oneness. As two people move towards the marriage commitment they have an optimum opportunity to discover whether the love they have for each other is truly 'love *full stop*', a love which sees but chooses to accept the negative traits they begin to discover within each other. Premature physical involvement clouds this growth process.

The third area of oneness between a man and a woman is obviously physical oneness—sexual intercourse. When sex is a consummation of the spiritual and soulish union which has gone before, it is the ultimately satisfying, explosive and creative sharing that everyone seeks but few experience. This is true sexual freedom. Any other path to it doesn't work. As John White has said, 'We live in a world where everything has a design and function. You don't set a fish free from the ocean (poor fish, so confined and restricted) or birds from the necessity of flight. Birds were designed to fly and fish to swim. They are freest when they are doing what they were designed to do. In the same way, your body was not designed for premarital sex and will never be truly free when you engage in it.'

As a relationship emphasizes the focus of spiritual growth and development for each person—as they individually draw closer in communication with God—they are automatically drawn closer to each other.

The experience of this truth in your romantic life will produce some of the most satisfying relationships you've ever enjoyed. In fact, you'll have to be a bit cautious at first that you don't mistake the euphoric 'spiritual' feelings you share with another person for true 'marital' love at last. They may be. But they could also be simply your first encounter with a man or a woman in a relationship as God intended it.

Before we explore some of the specific activities that can make these relationships such fun, we should look at one more basic pattern God built into men and women when he created them. God designed man to be the spiritual leader in marriage and woman to be the spiritual challenger or responder. The man's assignment is to provide a kind of leadership to which the woman can respond wholeheartedly. The roles are not competitive; they're complementary. He is to provide a leadership saturated with 'love *full stop*'. She is to be set free by this leadership to make a happy, reasoned and creative response. Contrary to the horror some in the women's liberation movement find in this idea, God's design provides for the fullest possible development of the personal worth, potential and uniqueness of both the man and the woman.

While a couple are going out, the man can begin to practise and understand godly initiation and leadership. And the woman can learn how to respond to a man. Obviously, if they have already decided to reserve sexual sharing for their life-long partner in marriage, thus eliminating it as a focus of tension while going out, their relationship can be truly free, fascinating and fun!

Amazingly, even today's 'sexually liberated' people who couldn't care less about the spiritual dimensions of life are learning that a friendship free of sexual games is very rewarding. In an April 1978 article for *Mademoiselle* magazine, Blair Sabol candidly related a conversation with a girlfriend who had expressed surprise that Blair hadn't gone to bed with her man on their second evening out. Blair commented,

> I was astounded. Here we had had what I thought was one of the most intimate evenings merely talking one-on-one and I had felt more satisfied in our sharing each other's personal war stories than in sharing a bed.... Before, I would have chalked off this evening as a failure because talking meant merely sparking a good friendship. And friendships supposedly were great to have, only between you and your dog. But between male and female, it usually meant once a friend, never a lover.... I am only interested in men I can...have a good conversation with.... Perhaps my new erogenous zone is my mind. Now I want my cerebrum stimulated.

Going out is fun when it provides a climate in which two people can become friends. Seeing a film the first time you go out, then, is generally counter-productive. There you sit for two hours, side by side in a darkened cinema, being entertained but never communicating. It's hardly the climate for getting to know one another. Save the films for later.

A better choice would be to go window-shopping together, or to visit a museum or exhibition, or take a walk in the park or round the zoo. Activities like these provide plenty to talk about and allow you to discover each other's tastes and backgrounds. You don't have to worry about being a good conversationalist, either; the topics of conversation are ready-made.

One of the most enjoyable 'dates' I ever had was visiting a cemetery. We had a hilarious time walking about, reading the comments on the old tombstones. It was a good time I'll never forget. And in case you're short on creative ideas for things to do, let me suggest a few. Some on the following list are quite common; others will catch your imagination. In either event, remember your own ideas will work the best for you. The best ideas are those which help you communicate and get to know each other more intimately. A good activity is one which helps you see and savour new delights and depths of one another's personalities. These ideas will also stimulate married couples who, hopefully, will never stop going out with each other.

- Play table games, work puzzles.
- Engage in simple sports like table tennis, croquet, or horseshoes.
- Go sailing, rowing, or swimming, or try other water sports.

- Take a walk through the neighbourhood, a shopping precinct, or a new housing estate.
- Do ordinary things together, like grocery shopping, going to the launderette, or gardening.
- Find some underprivileged children, orphans, or the kids next door and take them on an outing or picnic. Teach them a new craft or skill.
- Cook dinner together at her home or yours.
- Play sports like golf, tennis, squash, ten-pin bowling, roller- or ice-skating.
- Get involved in community ventures, a sponsored walk, or an aid project for the elderly or disadvantaged.
- Ride bicycles, play snooker, go brass-rubbing in local churches.
- Explore a local park or take a walk in the country.
- Pick a topic you both know nothing about and spend a couple of hours at the library discovering what you can.
- Identify the skills you'd like to learn from each other and take turns being the teacher.
- Tour some local industries and watch something being manufactured.
- Do crafts together. Make gifts and Christmas presents.
- Pick a theme and set out to take photographs in your area—interesting old buildings, doorknobs, children playing, unusual cars, elderly people, stained glass windows, or signs with odd messages.
- Build and fly a kite.
- Take a walk in the rain.
- Spend a Saturday tape-recording unusual sounds.
- Plan a party together and invite a collection of each other's friends.
- Think of a hard-to-find object and hunt for it.
- Haul out the family albums and get acquainted with each other's 'roots'.

- Go to church services and other church functions together.
- Take a train to a nearby town and go out for lunch or dinner.
- Go for a bus tour.
- Go to a play, concert, or ballet.
- Attend an auction.

These are only a small fraction of the activities that can make for great dates. For more ideas specific to your area, look in places like these:

- Ask your local tourist office for a list of the places worth visiting in your area.
- Check the local museums, colleges and library for a listing of forthcoming lectures, exhibits or attractions.
- Look in the 'coming events' section of your local newspaper.
- Ask your friends for their ideas.

As I indicated earlier, the best ideas are the ones you think up yourselves. Be creative. Let your imagination go free.

With these purposes and ideas for going out well in mind, let's talk for a moment about some of the common problems and rough spots. For example, I've met a lot of fellows and girls who complain that their partner, in an effort to be spiritual and keep things under control, spiritualizes everything. While I can appreciate the concern of such people, imbalance is never the best answer. If God's Spirit is alive in your life and Jesus Christ is important to you, it's only natural that you'll talk about it. But it probably isn't natural that this topic will consume the entire time you're together.

A lot of couples find that taking a moment to pray together is a beautiful way to begin and/or end a day out together. And mixing in activities which focus on mutually held spiritual values, commitments, or goals is an important facet of going out. After all, biblical values should be the core of life.

Another essential in a budding relationship is to involve your partner with your family and close friends. If the relationship grows into marriage you'll not only be marrying that individual, you'll be joining his or her family. If things are uncomfortable there, you'd better find out and understand why before you contemplate a permanent union. Observing how a person relates to his or her parents can reveal a lot about how well he or she handles intimate relationships and conflict in those relationships. What you learn now can save a lot of grief later.

And here's another suggestion which is especially useful if you're not interested in starting a relationship with any particular person, and yet you want to build some friendships with the opposite sex. If you are a girl, get together with a couple of your girlfriends and plan an evening or afternoon picnic; invite four or five men. Or vice versa, the men can get together and invite over some girls. Keep the numbers uneven to avoid the tension of having to pair up; plan just to have fun together.

One of the aspects of the culture in which you and I live is that anything goes. It can get us into trouble, but it has also produced a lot of new options in man-woman relationships. Women are free to use more initiative in such relationships. On balance this is a good thing. Sharing the expense of some activities no longer offends the old tough-guy image we men were expected to keep up. All of us are less role-conscious and more concerned about being aware and supportive human beings. In the dating relationship that's a great bonus.

Shortly after I became a Christian I started to go out with a Christian woman. After the sixth or seventh evening I felt I deserved something in return, so I started to make a little move with her. And she said no. I thought she was kidding, so I tried again. And she said no again! I was really annoyed, because not too many people had ever said no to me. So I said, 'Who do you think you are?' And she said, 'Who in the world do you think *you* are?' Right there, this liberated Christian woman began to teach me a lesson.

As I began to mature in my relationship with Christ, I began to realize that first of all, my companion was my sister in Christ. And there were a lot of things I used to do with a woman that I wouldn't do with my 'sister'. In fact, it wasn't long before this perspective broadened into an attitude of always thinking about how I could build up the woman I was with. How could I leave her a better individual because of the time we had spent together? Let me tell you, men and women, that when you go out with an attitude like that, it gets exciting. It's more fun than you've ever imagined.

It is pure joy when you treat someone you go out with as you would treat the individual you will someday marry. You won't find a better way to love your girlfriend or boyfriend or the man or woman he or she will eventually marry. And you'll be doing yourself an enormous favour in the process. You'll be learning how to love better, with God's divine 'I love you *full stop*' love. You'll be growing into the 'right' kind of person—one to whom God can entrust his prized son or daughter as your marriage partner for life.

Is that promise worth the commitment? Is this reward worth the work and the wait? Let's weigh the cost.

# 9

# *The Secret of Loving*

A well-known actor, famous for his romantic roles, was being interviewed on a television chat show. The host asked what skills he considered essential for being a 'great lover'. The star's reply was as surprising as it was profound: 'A great lover is someone who can satisfy one woman for all her life, and who can be satisfied by one woman all his life long. A great lover isn't someone who goes from woman to woman. Any dog can do that.'

By now it should be quite clear that I believe the secret of loving to be first of all possessing and sharing God's 'I love you *full stop*' love. Secondly, it is becoming a mature person through the growth experiences of life so that at the right moment, in the right relationship, God can bring you to the right person—one who can uniquely complement you. And finally, the secret of loving is sharing intimately with your partner, in the security of the marriage relationship, the ultimate expression of your many-faceted love—sexual intercourse.

Quite simply, that's the goal. That's the game plan. That's what we should aim for. So why is something so simple, profound, and appealing so difficult? Why is the path to the goal so littered with the carnage of individual lives and relationships that didn't make it? Why have so many fine people become sidetracked?

There are several important reasons and I want you to look at four of them. Think of them as the four 'D's'.

The first is *daft*. Some people are mindless, stupid, and daft about love and sex. They wander blindly into a situation unaware of the consequences. And before they wake up to what is happening, they are ambushed.

We teach children that to play with fire is to be burned, that to run in front of a speeding car is to be killed. The same warning needs to be given in the realm of love and sex. If we use poor judgement, if we base our lives on principles that aren't true, if we violate the function and purposes God intended for sex, then we reap the results. The usual results are a lot of hurt and pain, and a diluted, if not ruined relationship. Being daft is no excuse. God has given each of us a mind and the ability to use it. To wander carelessly and mindlessly into the danger-filled arena of sex—letting your glands be your guide—is stupid. Ignorantly wading into the swamp is a great way to find yourself up to your neck in crocodiles.

Reason two is *deliberate*. There are a lot of people who pride themselves on having brains. 'Daft I am not' is their motto. This person knows what God says, but deliberately decides to follow his own desires. He's too smart to get caught in the consequences. Or so he thinks. Of course he knows what the Bible promises—both positive and negative—but

Mr Deliberate has decided that he's a special case. Whatever is supposed to happen only happens to the other fellow. 'It won't happen to me, I'm special. I won't get hurt. I won't get V.D. I won't ruin my future. I won't get a girl pregnant. I'm cool. I'm smarter than the average bear. I can play with fire and not get burned.'

There's only one problem with this point of view— it never works. No amount of wishful thinking can alter the principles and priorities God programmed into you and me. The consequences of these principles are as certain as the sexual drives we are seeking to satisfy if we violate them. Oh, we may seem to be getting away with it—for a while. But deliberately avoiding God's way ultimately leads to disaster. Always!

There's a third reason: *distractions and lack of discernment*. As we saw in chapter 2, we're constantly bombarded with information overload in the area of sex. Some stimuli are stronger than others. But regardless how blatant or subtle the message, the point is always the same. 'You are a person who has the right to sexual fulfilment. Do what feels good. It's wrong for anyone, even God, to tell you not to.'

Writer Tom Wolfe called the seventies the 'Me Decade', and the eighties don't look much different. Everything is focused on *me*, what *I* need and what *I* want. Others have called it the age of narcissism—a term taken from the Greek legend in which a young man became so enthralled with his reflection in a pool of water that he did not take time to eat or drink, and wasted away into death. That's what I think many of us are doing today. We're so enthralled with ourselves that we're dying instead of living.

This 'age of narcissism' pumps out the 'me' messages. Whether it's self-help books or the less direct messages emitted by television programmes and adverts, we're bombarded with sexual images and the theme, 'If it feels good, do it. You're responsible to no one but yourself.'

Because we cannot totally escape from our culture, it's important that we develop discernment. One way is to balance the negative messages you receive with positive ones from God's word. I have a friend who writes film reviews for magazines. Over the past six months he has become aware of the subtle influences on his mind and values exercised by the secular messages proclaimed in films. He doesn't spend his time reviewing X-rated films, but he's aware that the world's viewpoint on sex is very permissive. And my friend has learned that if he's going to continue to see and review some seventy films a year, he's going to have to spend a proportionate amount of time in extra Bible study and Christian fellowship. Balance is essential. We need to fill our minds with the good in order to survive sexually in the current self-seeking age.

The fourth big reason why people get sidetracked is *desire and lack of discipline*. Probably the most common reason for wandering off God's path is that the benefits of waiting seem so distant and the pleasures of indulging are so immediate. Let's face it, sex can be enjoyable outside marriage—the passionate foreplay, the explosive climax, the feelings of conquering and/or manipulating your lover. I've met couples who sincerely feel that they love each other with a 'love *full stop*' love, and who are committed to each other outside marriage. But I'm convinced from the encounters I've had with thousands of these young people, and from what I've read in Scripture, that the long-term results are negative. Whether it's guilt, remorse, or plain sadness that accompanies a break-up with that 'committed partner', the long-term results of sex outside marriage are nothing compared to the benefits that can be enjoyed in the context of marital love.

The problem is that it takes self-discipline to wait. And many of us are unpractised in the art of discipline. We may have disciplined ourselves for months when we took piano lessons or practised football, but as we've aged we've been snared by the emphasis on instant gratification.

What is the secret of discipline? There are no easy answers, but I'll give you a couple of *simple* ones. One is to concentrate on the goals you desire for your marriage. Visualize them. Talk about them. Write them down and review them often. You'll find your actions conforming to your talk, writing and imagination. The opposite is also true. If you write, talk and visualize 'making it' with everyone you go out with, you'll find your body heading without complaint in that direction. Social scientists call this teleology—the principle of goals leading to actions.

A second suggestion is to keep your mind on Christ and on his words as much as possible. The more closely you walk with Christ, the more self-disciplined you become. The more intimate your relationship with him, the more you try to please him and the less time and energy you spend on your own urges. The apostle James comments on this in the Bible: 'Submit therefore to God. Resist the devil and he will flee from you. Draw near to God and He will draw near to you' (James 4:7-8). I've discovered that the more closely you walk with God, the more direction and self-discipline he gives you.

Sexual desire and intensity will modify somewhat as you grow older, but the need for self-discipline in many areas of life will continue. Earlier I alluded to the fact that sex is only one-twelfth of the marriage relationship. Let me give you a little more insight on this. In July of 1978 *Ebony* magazine interviewed a variety of couples on the topic of 'Sex in Marriage'. Here's what some of them said:

Dr and Mrs Richard Tyson, co-directors of the Institute for Marriage Enrichment and Sexual Studies in America, said,

> Sex cannot be separated from the other elements in the total relationship. Sex is important throughout a marriage, though it seems that quantity is more important in the early years. But as time goes by and the relationship begins to mature, quality sex seems more important to couples. A couple may have sex ten times a week, and it may be lousy for the woman and great for the man. She would probably rather have one good sexual relationship a week.

Roebuck 'Pop' Staples has been married to his wife Oceola for forty-three years. He said,

> Sex plays a big and a good part in a happy marriage, but no marriage can make it off sex and sex alone. You've got to have more than that. The first thing you've got to have is understanding; another is respect. You've got to care for and love each other. But I don't know how you can make it if you are not sexually compatible. A man and a woman have got to send out

some vibes to each other; you've got to have good sex in a marriage. A lot of young people think sex is all there is to marriage, but after they see what's happening, they realize that a lot of other things are equally important.

Another excellent observation came from Shirley Robinson, a Christian wife, who said,

Marriage must be based on friendship and love, and if God is first in your life, all other things will fall into place. Because my husband and I are so compatible in so many ways, we have a very good sex life. There is no problem of communication as there is in many unions. We are able to talk freely about sex or anything else, and this is important to us. A good marriage is not based on physical love and beauty alone. What if a mate becomes physically incapacitated or disfigured? A good marriage can weather such storms and still find sunshine.

The point is made: the quantity of sex may diminish over the years, but the need for quality will continue. To have quality sex you must have love, patience and self-discipline—the desire to give rather than to get. Desires may abate; the need for self-discipline never does. And the patterns of self-discipline which will later give you sensitive, dynamic and fulfilling sex are the patterns you are building right now in your pre-marital relationships.

In looking at these reasons why we fail to achieve what God intended for us in love and sex, we see many negatives: being *daft*; a *deliberate* flaunting of God's design; *distractions and lack of discernment;* overwhelming *desires and lack of self-discipline*. But let me assure you that these negatives can turn into positives.

If there's one positive statement I would want you to retain, it's this: God loves you. Jesus came to prove it and to clear sin out of the way, so that we could experience God's highest desire for us—an abundant and ultimately fulfilling life. He wants us to know his love daily and personally—to enjoy it and share it with others. And he wants us to mature in the way he originally intended us to. He has communicated to us his principles of conduct to protect and provide for our welfare.

He has even gone so far as to take care of our failures when we confess them and accept his forgiveness. Through a personal relationship with Jesus Christ, we become transformed. Our minds are renewed. We are changed. We no longer have to be daft, or deliberately disobedient, or distracted, or destitute of discipline. We are set free to love and serve and live an unparalleled life, whether it's in the bedroom or any other room of life.

That's the secret of loving. There is no other.

Don't miss out.